A Pony Named Trigger
   Copyright 2018 ©

By Claire Hudgins Christa

Illustrations by Lisa Cantrell

Thank you to my daughter, Caitlin Christa, who is the whole reason I wrote this book about my beloved childhood pony. Thank you to my husband, Mike, who encourages me always to follow my dreams. Thanks to my daughter Connor who loves to read, which inspired me to publish a book that I know I would have read as a child. Thank you to my parents and grandparents who raised me amongst fields of green pastures and horses and my brother Richard Talbot Hudgins for teaching Trigger to be the good little pony he turned out to be.

Cover illustration and sketches by Lisa Shaw Cantrell, a dear friend and fellow horse lover. Thank you for taking time out of your busy schedule to sketch these amazing pictures of my feisty and fun pony.

A Pony Named Trigger

It is a cool, crisp morning somewhere between fall and winter. There is a frost on the ground that glistens in the rising sunshine. The horses in the pasture know that they will soon hear the sound of grain pouring into the big, plastic buckets. They whinny in anticipation.

The first to come from
the lower pasture is always the
little black and white pony.
The humans call him Trigger,
but he has always felt that
a more brave and fierce name
would be more suitable. He
is faster than all of the other
horses in the pasture, and
smarter too.

He knows not to come up too quickly lest the human with the bucket has one of those leather strappy things to catch him with again. He is covered in dust and grass from rolling in the green pastures. His mane is tangled and the whiskers on his muzzle are long and wiry from the carefree days out in the fields.

He wonders what the day will hold. Would the human allow him to enjoy his bucket of grain in peace today or will there be a price to pay for his meal? He prances toward the bucket, ears perked and tail held high in the air.

He hesitantly moves forward, looking closely for that thing that the humans always carry when they want to interrupt his plans and take him from the other horses. The coast looks clear so he immerses his head into the delicious bucket of food. The green grass of the pasture is delightful, but oh how much better is the sweet taste of grain!

All of a sudden the leather strap goes around his neck. He leaps backward. He feels a tight pull on his neck. He drags the human forward. The human pulls back. He has been tricked. He has been caught. Trigger knows what is next. The dreadful metal thing in his mouth that forces him to turn this way or that, and often not in the direction he wishes to go. The human allows him to finish his grain but now the taste is just not as sweet.

He endures the brushing
and detangling of his mane.
He secretly enjoys the brush
on his back and neck. The
cleaning out of his hooves
is quite unpleasant but then
he is relieved to feel the
dislodging of the rock that
has been stuck in the frog
of his hoof for some time now.

He puts back his ears in protest and swings his neck around to nip at the human as the big, heavy leather thing hits his back. The human swats his muzzle and he feels slightly ashamed. He resolves himself to a day of extra weight on his back, the metal thing in his mouth, and time away from his friends.

He wonders where they will go today. They seem to be heading to his favorite spot. Yes, he knows the road well. They are going to the open fields with the bubbling creek that twists it's way through the middle. Oh, how he loves this place. He snickers to himself recalling the many times he has laid down in the middle of the creek and has forced the human to jump off of his back as he proceeded to roll in the cool, refreshing water.

He is also pleased with the time he was able to make her fall off in the soft green grass, enabling him to run and prance through those open fields weightless and free. He contemplates pulling one of those stunts once more.

Then he feels his human petting his neck and hears her calling him a good boy. He knows this to be true, but is glad that she is acknowledging it. He decides that today he will allow her to stay on his back. "Yes," he thinks to himself, "Just for today I will let her stay on."

The End

If you enjoyed this story about Trigger, please tell a friend. Be on the look out for more stories about my adventures with my favorite pony. Thank you!

The book is available for sale on Amazon.com and Kindle.

www.ingramcontent.com/pod-product-compliance
Lightning Source LLC
Chambersburg PA
CBHW031440040426
42444CB00006B/909